2012

Barbara

WITH ALL MY HEART

WITH ALL MY
HEART

❧ CINDIE TRIEBER ❧

North Valley Publications
3530 De La Cruz Boulevard
Santa Clara, CA 95054
408.988.8881
nvpublications.org

Edited by Crissi Hussin, Sarah Uson, Jo Winn, and Nathan Winn
Cover Design by Jad Limcaco
Layout by Nathan Winn

ISBN: 978-1-60171-692-7

Printed in the United States of America

DEDICATION

This book is dedicated with love to my husband Jack, my best friend and husband of thirty-eight years; as well as to my children: Tiffany, Tim, and Tabitha and their mates: Ryan, Rebecca, and Chris. Also to those precious grandchildren who call me Nana: Ashlyn, Titus, TJ, Riley, Hudson, Rhegan, Landon, and the soon-to-be Thompson baby who will join our family in January 2012. You are my joy, my life, and the real reason I wrote this book. I love you.

ACKNOWLEDGEMENTS

To my parents, Melvin and Geraldine Swanson for bringing me up in the nurture and admonition of the Lord. Thank you for your deep and faithful commitment to God and to your family. I love you.

To my six brothers and my sister, DeWayne, Rich, Kelvin, Doug, Mark, Vennie, and Verlyn. Thank you for your encouragement and for the lives we shared together growing up in the Swanson household. I love you.

To the North Valley Baptist Church, thank you for loving me as a young and inexperienced pastor's wife and for being a constant source of blessing and encouragement to me. I love you.

To Nathan and Jo Winn, thank you for your enthusiasm and positive input. Without your help, this book would never have been written. Thank you for your hours and hours of editing, proofreading, and typesetting. You are treasures to our ministry. Thank you for bearing the load of this book. I love you both.

TABLE OF CONTENTS

FOREWORD

—————————— ∽ ——————————

WITH ALL MY HEART IS AN EXTRAORDINARY literary journey in the life of the most wonderful lady in the world—Cindie Swanson Trieber. Chapter by chapter is filled with details of our life together, beginning on December 23, 1972, when we were married. Next to my salvation, asking Cindie to be my wife has been the greatest decision of my life. She has been my friend, "help meet," completer, and encourager. She believed in me when I certainly did not believe in myself.

In addition to being an amazing wife, Cindie has also been an incredible mother to our three children—Tiffany, Timothy, and Tabitha, who are now raising children of their own, guided by the godly principles they learned in their youth. Cindie and I are grandparents to seven (soon to be eight) grandchildren as well.

For the past many years, Cindie has been the ideal pastor's wife—there is none better. She knows how to accomplish the task, thus being a constant blessing to me and to the church family of the North Valley Baptist Church. This ministry has truly been strengthened because of the godliness, compassion, and sincerity of this great lady; and I believe that this book will imprint your life as her life has imprinted ours.

Cindie, I love you so much. I am proud of you and honored to be called your husband. God bless you.

Dr. Jack Trieber
Pastor, North Valley Baptist Church

INTRODUCTION

GROWING UP IN A CHRISTIAN HOME IS certainly a privilege, but growing up in the Trieber home, simply stated, was growing up in heaven on earth. I hold countless memories in my heart and mind that were created during my childhood. Without a doubt, my mother played a crucial role in creating our home a haven. The atmosphere was sweet, kind, loving, and always a place where we could share our hearts. I am indebted to my mom for the desire she placed inside of me, at a very young age, to be a wife and mother. The Lord places people in your life that will forever make an imprint. For me, God placed a Proverbs 31 lady whom I call "Mom." I watched her as she maintained a consistent walk with God, as she taught and trained us how young ladies should act, and how she served her Lord both when the sun was shining and when the days were full of dark clouds.

I am excited as you read in these pages how to love your God, your husband, and your children. You will catch a glimpse of the rare treasure that God allowed to be my mother.

Mom, I love you! I admire you for your example, your love for Dad, children, grandchildren, and church family. You are truly amazing, and I love you . . . with all my heart!

—Tiffany (Trieber) Thompson

THE QUESTION BEING EXAMINED IN Proverbs 31 is, "Who can find a virtuous woman?" As we look at the overwhelming majority of ladies in our nation, we come to the conclusion that the virtuous woman is the minority. As the son of Mrs. Cindie Trieber, I can sincerely say that she truly is a virtuous woman. My mom has selflessly given of her time, talents, and treasures to her husband, children, ministry, and God.

Throughout this book, you will find practical advice regarding effective ministry, maintaining a healthy home, and achieving a happy marriage. The contents within the pages of this book have been proven time and time again. It gives me great joy to encourage you as you read "With All My Heart."

—Tim Trieber

∽

"HER CHILDREN ARISE UP, AND CALL HER blessed" (Proverbs 31:28). Having been raised in the home of Cindie Trieber, I can say, without a doubt, that she fits the description of a Proverbs 31 woman. By her life, she has imparted to me and displayed what it is to be a Christian, a wife, and a mother. I wanted nothing more than to be a wife and mother just like her. I am so thankful for the privilege I have of calling her "Mama." She has been the greatest giver I have ever known, even going without to make sure her family was cared for. Our family calls her "Super Nana" because she throws her life into her grandkids.

My mom makes the lives of those she comes in contact with brighter. She has been a perfect pastor's wife and thrown herself into the ministry. Her realness is one of my favorite qualities she possesses—whether at home or at church, she is always the same. She has molded me into the wife and mother I am, and I strive every day to follow her example. I am so excited about this book becoming reality. I know it will be a blessing and help to each one who reads it.

—Tabitha (Trieber) Fanara

WITH ALL MY
HEART

She looketh well to the ways of her household,
and eateth not the bread of idleness.

—PROVERBS 31:27

CHAPTER ONE

———————— ᔰ ————————

Creating a Haven

IS LIFE EVER NOT BUSY? WITH ALL THE festivities of the year's holidays, it is so easy for us women to stress out, and in the attempt to make everything "just perfect" for our families, we "endure" the seasons rather than enjoy them. I hope that you were able to enjoy all that the last Christmas season brought to your home. I try to make the best of each season and make it the special time that my family deserves. I always get so thankful when Thanksgiving and Christmas decorations are packed away and it is apparent that Valentine's Day is fast approaching in our home! I love the season when "love is in the air!"

As each new year rolls around, I hope that you take the time you need to make your usual "list" of New

Year's resolutions. One New Years, I was visiting with my sister, and I made the comment to her that I wasn't establishing resolutions that year because then I didn't have to feel guilty when I didn't keep them! Have you ever been there? Nonetheless, I try to make my lists of goals and ambitions for each new year, and I am sure that you do as well. As busy wives, mothers, and church members, we need to do all that we can to make certain our homes and lives are operating "decently and in order" as we are commanded in God's word. Some of the ideas listed below might help you as they have helped me to effectively run my home.

. . .

Complete Your Calendar

Make sure that the calendar (your control center) is completed and placed where all of the members of the family can see it. Be sure to mark down every birthday, anniversary, and event that you know is going to take place. Don't miss a child's birthday because you failed to plan.

Set Goals

It is better to shoot for the moon and hit the street light than to never shoot at all. If it is the perpetual diet that you need to work on, then work on it. We Americans are too overweight. Feasting on sweets and junk food will destroy the temples God has given us. Get some good reading material on health, and put into practice what you read.

Determine What Is Important
Each evening before going to bed, make a list of what you need to do tomorrow. List items according to priority.

Prevent Interruptions
Most people are interrupted at least once every five minutes. If your calendar is posted and the menu is on the refrigerator door, it can save you having to answer a lot of questions like, "What's going on tonight?" or "What are we having for dinner?"

Get in Order
Go through and sort out items that you do not use. Don't be a packrat! Organization is the key to a well-run household. Remember that a home out of order is a life out of order.

Designate Areas
Store your keys, glasses, and important items in a designated area. I always leave my keys in the car in the garage, or I hang them up on the key ring near the exit

door. I keep sunglasses in a basket on a shelf close to the door as well. I can remember one year while I was packing away Christmas decorations, I temporarily lost my car keys. After going through several bags of garbage and scouring the house, I found them on the kitchen table in the centerpiece! From that time one, I decided that I would always put things in a designated location.

Cut Calls

Cut unwanted calls short. These calls can really use up valuable time.

Plan Errands

There is no need to run to Target and the grocery store several times a week. Make an organized and itemized list of what you need, and take it with you.

Stop Procrastinating

Do first what you like to do the least! If it is folding that load of white laundry, do that first!

Just Do It

Everything doesn't have to be perfect. I like perfection as well as the next person, but I am usually the only one that can really tell if that small area I am stressing about is perfect or not. Some jobs don't need perfection as much as they just need to be done!

Combine Tasks

Do more than one thing at a time. You can read while you run on the treadmill, make lists while you wait at a stop light, or talk on the phone while you cook!

Control Your Time

Become a person who takes control of your time—don't let time control you.

Keep Trying

Remember: If at first you don't succeed, try, try again.

Plan Ahead

Plan a vacation with your family. Start saving money so that you will have a great time. You don't need an enormous amount of money to have fun, but you will need an adequate amount.

Make Prayer a Priority

Buy a new prayer journal, and make this year's quiet time with God the best.

Shop Now

Take advantage of the after-holiday sales, and buy special gifts ahead of time.

Decorate for the Seasons

If Christmas is the only holiday for which you decorate, change that this year. Decorate now for the upcoming holiday. Make it fun!

Are there things you wish you had done differently last year? Now is your chance. You have a clean slate. Make it happen this year.

She stretcheth out her hand to the poor; yea, she reacheth forth her hands to the needy.

—PROVERBS 31:20

———— ∽ ————

CHAPTER TWO

Giving, An Expression of Love

JOY—JESUS, OTHERS, AND YOU. REAL JOY always comes from putting others first and caring for the needs of others before our own. Yet, if we are not careful to plan how we can daily give to others, we will forget or become too busy. Have you ever heard the saying, "Plan your work, and work your plan"? How true it is. If you haven't sat down and planned out your calendar, do it now. It's not too late. Your life will be more productive and your household will run more smoothly if you plan ahead.

Loving and giving to others is, most often, associated with the month of February and Valentine's Day. It is the month that we are to express our love to those who mean so much to us, even though we should do this every day.

Make the 14th of February a special day for your family. If you do not have family nearby, make it special for someone else. We need to teach by our example. Children will do as they are taught. If they see you reach out to others with compassion and demonstrate acts of kindness that make people feel valued, loved and significant, they will do so as well. Plan now to make the day great. Buy those cards and special gifts. Don't let February the 14th come and go without making it the special day it was intended to be. Maybe you really blew it last year, so why not recover this year? Go ahead; you will be glad you did.

We find in Webster's Dictionary . . .

---

love   [luhv]

noun
1 strong affection
2 warm attachment
3 beloved person
4 unselfish, loyal, and benevolent concern for others
5 a score of zero in tennis

While most of us chuckle at the last definition, many have scored a zero—but that zero is in the area of love. How sad to live a life that has very little or no love. I cannot imagine my life if I did not feel loved by those closest to me—my husband, my children, and my church family. Although I enjoy Valentine's Day as most of you do, should we not be showing love every day of the year all year long? I have listed some tips below that I believe will help you to make every month special, as well as planning ahead to Valentine's Day. Because as our pastor says, "Love is always demonstrated."

- Make sure you tell your loved ones "I love you" every day.

- Do something special every day this month to show your love. For example, give a compliment every day. (Don't be surprised if the recipient acts shocked.)

- Make Valentine's Day special by planning ahead, and remember, it is on the same day every year.

- Decorate your house. There are so many cute decorations available.

- Make a special breakfast. You could make heart-shaped French toast and set the table with all red and white dishes.

- Apply toothpaste on everyone's toothbrush and turn down their beds for them before they retire for the night.

- Make Valentine's cards with your children.

- Do something special for your mate that only you can do.

▸ Show special love for your pastor and your church.

▸ Remember to tell someone about the greatest love of all, knowing Jesus Christ as his personal Savior.

· · ·

Who will be in heaven because you took the time to tell him how he could know that heaven could be his eternal home? Simply share your testimony with people and explain how they can know for sure about heaven. The greatest gift of love ever given was God's son, Jesus. He left all of heaven's glory and was nailed to a rugged cross to die for us. What love! Did you tell someone today about Jesus? If not, plan to do so tomorrow. His story is truly the greatest love story ever written.

Someone once said, "We make a living by what we get; we make a life by what we give." How are you doing in the giving department? Start now . . . today, not tomorrow or next month.

Giving to Your Church

In the month of February, the North Valley Baptist Church always enjoys a special day called "I Love My Church" Sunday. Let me ask you this: do you really love your church? If so, what are you doing to further the cause of Christ through your local church? Let me give you a few suggestions that I believe will be a help to you as you give to your church.

- *Be faithful to your church.* Attendance should never be a question. If you want your children to live for God, you cannot bypass the church.

- *Pray for your pastor daily.* Become his prayer warrior. Make it a point to daily offer his name to the Lord.

- *Be involved in your church.* You do not have to be an usher, bus driver, Sunday school teacher, choir member, and nursery worker all at the same time. Take on one ministry, and do it to the best of your ability. We have "starters" and "stoppers" because people allow themselves to get too busy; when that happens, they end up not doing anything well— and they usually "stop" doing everything due to frustration.

- *Plan ahead.* If you keep the church activities on your calendar and plan ahead, you will not be prone to complain about being "busy."

- *Be faithful with your tithe.* I would be afraid not to tithe. God always gets it back, whether it is in doctor bills, car problems, or even financial reversal.

▸ *Be an encouragement to those around you.* Write notes often, compliment others, and put a smile on your face.

▸ *Never let anyone talk negatively about your church.* Don't allow yourself to listen to anyone who speaks ill of your church. God has ordained the church and the office of the pastor. It's your job to support him, not let people tear him down.

▸ *Invite your neighbors to go to church with you.* Do your neighbors even know you attend church?

▸ *Bring your Bible and something on which to take notes.* Your pastor gives a wealth of great truths that can help you. Don't trust your memory to remember all that was said.

▸ *Pray for your church every day.* The more you pray for your church, the more you will want to become involved.

Leading with the Heart

Our hearts are vital organs; in fact, our bodies couldn't exist without them. We will never be good "givers" if our hearts aren't in good condition. Have you ever noticed how self focused we become when our hearts aren't right? We can never be consumed with expressing love to those around us by giving if our hearts aren't in the right place. Having the right heart is of utmost importance as we serve the King of kings.

▸ *Have a sanctified heart.* Develop a pure heart where sin is confessed daily, and a holy life is your desire.

▸ *Have a servant's heart.* Being a servant isn't lowly; it is the ultimate measure of greatness.

▸ *Have a submissive heart.* While we stutter and cringe at the word "submission," remember that, "Submission doesn't bring you bondage; it brings you freedom."

▸ *Have a sacrificial heart.* What can I do for someone else? Whom can I serve today? Give of yourself to build someone else.

Life has its ups and downs, but giving from the heart will always prove to be rewarding in the long run.

*O love the L*ORD*, all ye his saints: for the* LORD *preserveth the faithful, and plentifully rewardeth the proud doer.*

—PSALM 31:23

CHAPTER THREE

~

Remembering When

IT WAS ON MARCH 1, 1976 THAT BRO. TRIEBER and I came to North Valley Baptist Church. Wow, where has the time gone? We were just young kids when we arrived at North Valley! And, to say "a lot of water has gone under the bridge" would be an understatement. I would never have imagined that God would take that small band of people when we arrived and make our church what it is today. So many memories flood my mind. We didn't have children when we came to North Valley, and now we are blessed with not only three children but also two sons-in-law, a daughter-in-law, and seven adorable grandchildren (with one on the way) that call us "Nana" and "Papa!" Many of our church members have been with us since day one, and a large delegation has been here for a decade or more. We are so blessed and thankful. Our love for our church is far greater today than it was back then.

This chapter will permit me neither the time nor space to reflect on all the memories that I have in my memory bank. Yet, when I look at pictures and videos of years past, I am reminded of where our church has been and where we are today. From a small A-frame building, to a well-furnished tent, and several building projects later, we have a beautiful campus just a few blocks from the property where it all started. I am so thankful for the faithfulness of my husband and for the members who have been with us during these wonderful and exciting years. God has been so good to us!

It is because our people have been faithful to the Lord that He, in turn, has blessed us and allowed us to thrive. I know for sure that if our church hadn't, under the leadership of their pastor, been faithful and obedient to the Lord, I would not have so many wonderful years to look back on.

. . .

I can recall a special event in our church trying to get church members to the house of God on a weekly basis. For a month we asked members to pull out all the stops and get to Sunday school. Looking back on those years, I have asked myself this question; "Why do we seemingly have to beg and bribe people to get to Sunday school? Is it not our reasonable service to get to church as God's children?" While we all have sat through a Sunday school lesson or two that may have lulled us to sleep, I'm sure that we can also testify that we learn so much if we come with an open heart and just listen. Here are some ideas that have helped our church.

▸ Pray for your Sunday school teacher and your pastor every day.

▸ Pray for your own Sunday school class, your church, and its members.

▸ Bring your Bible and something with which to take notes.

▸ Get to bed at an early hour on Saturday night so you will not drift off to sleep while your teacher or pastor is pouring out his heart.

▸ Get to God's house on time. Some people come to Sunday school so late they have missed over half of the lesson.

▸ If you are a wife and mother, make sure that everything is ready for Sunday morning. Pastor Trieber has often made reference to this in his preaching on the home. Pack the diaper bag on Saturday night. Make sure that all the clothes are ironed and ready for Sunday morning.

▸ Wake up the family to good, upbeat Christian music on Sunday morning.

▸ Don't let the devil cause division between you and your family on Sunday morning. (You have six other days for this!)

▸ Bring a smile with you, and be an encouragement to those you meet on Sunday morning.

▸ Invite someone to come with you to your class. Tell them you have the best teacher in the world.

▸ Don't miss more than two to three Sundays per year. If everyone in your class were just like you, what would your Sunday school class be like?

• • •

Perhaps you sang this chorus when you were young like I did:

"Everybody ought to go to Sunday school,
Sunday school, Sunday school,
The mamas and the papas and the boys and the girls,
Everybody ought to go to Sunday school."

You will really have a spring in your step and a song in your heart if you will apply the ideas listed above and follow the truth in this little chorus. In reflecting back about the faithfulness of our church, I can point to these few areas that our church has made priority, allowing us to receive the blessings of the Lord.

Train up a child in the way he should go: and when he is old, he will not depart from it.

—PROVERBS 22:6

CHAPTER FOUR

Raising the Next Generation

WE OFTEN HEAR THE PHRASE "APRIL showers bring May flowers," and that is definitely true. Yet, as Christians, we have other "showers" that we can reflect on—specifically, "showers of blessings." It never ceases to amaze me just how good God has been and continues to be to me!

When I think of blessings, my mind wanders back to those wonderful years when our children were in our home. All of our children are now married, and we are, and most likely will always be, in a perpetual state of experiencing the "empty nest syndrome." What started out as a journey with just my husband and me has evolved into a wonderful life with more than a dozen of us. It went so fast. I remember days filled with so many activities that I climbed into bed many a night completely exhausted. For those of you living in the busy days of parenthood, let me remind you that "your today will soon be your yesterday." Please let me reiterate to you the importance of enjoying these days, and not just enduring them. I am happy to say that, as I look back, I may have changed a few things if I could do it all over again—but I don't regret one mile. The older your children become, you will realize more and more that you have only one chance at this thing called parenting. Through the years, I have held to a few principles to guide me as I tried to raise my children while they were young. Please allow God to use these in your life.

Get Your Priorities in Order

Attitudes as well as actions say, "Look, kid, you are a hindrance to my work." Children do not want to play second fiddle to a parent's work. Remember the order is: God, spouse, children, work, church. I know that, as a provider for the home, work is top of the list for a man, but, it should never take important time away from your children.

Live Consistently

God doesn't expect you to be perfect, but He wants to be perfect through you.

Confess Your Failures
When you've made a mistake, admit it! You will be setting a good example of honesty for your children to follow.

Communicate
Keep the channels of communication open. Anger, frustration, constant preaching, and sarcasm are surefire ways to stop the flow of communication.

Go Easy with Your Criticism
You will drive your children from you with constant criticism. Instead, provide them with compliments, seasoned with praise.

Let Your Child Be Himself
Clothes and styles that seem "trendy" to us don't last too long. Don't forget that your era is outdated. I realize that modesty is always in style, but as Marlene Evans said so often, "If it isn't wrong, wicked, or against the Bible, leave them alone." That helped me so much as a mother.

Build a Fence of Prayer
Surround your children with a fence of prayer. Ask God to guide, direct, and protect them. My mind has been filled with so many "what ifs" since my son Tim was involved in a hit-and-run accident one Sunday night

while taking some teen bus boys home. Even though the car he was driving was literally a wreck, the outcome could have been so much worse. Yet, everyone in the car walked away with no major injuries. I am thankful that my prayer every day is for protection for my children.

Leave Them

Once your child has joined his/her partner in marriage, help them to "leave" you (Genesis 2:24). Yes, I am getting to practice what I preach.

Listen More Than You Lecture

A discussion is always more pleasant than a lecture, so do whatever is necessary to keep from preaching a sermon every time one of your children says something that sets off your alarm.

Realize God's Love

Realize that God loves and cares for your children more than you do. As a parent, that is hard to comprehend; but it is true. If we have done all that we possibly can with God's help, leave the results with God.

• • •

When my oldest daughter Tiffany was a senior in high school in 1997, the school theme song that year was, "My Life, Lord, Is Yours to Control." That song has been my theme for my children. The chorus says this:

> *"My life, Lord, is Yours to control;*
> *I give You my heart and my soul.*
> *I'll seek Your will, never mine,*
> *Rich treasures to find.*
> *Give wisdom to choices I make,*
> *Along every path that I take,*
> *So when I complete life's race,*
> *'Well done,' You will say."*

My children and your children all have a race to run. Let's help them make it to the finish line. If you seek Him first, God will bless you as you rear your children for His glory. And, it will be "yesterday" before you know it.

While They Are Young

There is nothing as fulfilling and exhilarating, and there is nothing so depleting and exhausting as parenting. It's the best of jobs. It is the most difficult of jobs. It brings us great joy, and it can also cause us the greatest pain. Parenting means hard work, pain, and tears; but, never forget, God intended for women to have joy and satisfaction through children. The calling of motherhood is a high calling. I am thankful I was able to be home with my children. The family is more important than the family room, the love is more important than the loveseat, and the bedtime story is more important than the bed. As mothers raising our children, it is our responsibility to bring them up in the nurture and admonition of the Lord and see to it that some things are provided for them in our homes while they are still young children.

1. Provide a refuge . . .

- ‣ where children run to and not from.

- ‣ where the everyday anxieties of life can be calmed. Don't stress your children by making them be overly involved!

- ‣ where feelings are mended. Did you know your children have feelings too?

- ‣ where your children know they are loved.

2. Provide a classroom . . .

- ‣ where values of life are taught.

- ‣ where instruction in manners is given.

- ‣ where discipline is administered properly.

- ‣ where help in education is obtained.

- ‣ where respect for authority is learned.

3. Provide a work place . . .

- ▸ where you teach your children to work. *(instruction)*

- ▸ where you show them how to work. *(demonstration)*

- ▸ where you correct mistakes they make in working. *(inspection)*

- ▸ where you praise them for their work. *(admiration)*

- ▸ where you let your children know that life is not all about fun—you must teach them that they will always have responsibilities.

4. Provide a place of fun . . .

- ▸ and spend fun time with your children.

- ▸ and plan activities for your children (bike and car rides, birthday parties, vacations, popcorn and a film, baseball games, etc.).

- ▸ and leave the work once in a while to go play.

5. Provide a spiritual place . . .

- ▸ where you teach them they need a Savior.

- ▸ where you practice the presence of Jesus in your home.

- ▸ where your family spends time together with God.

- ▸ where you pray with your children.

- ▸ where your family supports your church and your pastor.

Raising children is an awesome responsibility, and it is beyond our human abilities. God will give you the strength and patience you need as you seek Him in your parenting. Let me encourage you with this thought: They do grow up and give you grandchildren, so the best is yet to come!

He that gathereth in summer is a wise son: but he that sleepeth in harvest is a son that causeth shame.

—Proverbs 10:5

CHAPTER FIVE

Summer Schedule

BUSY, BUSY, BUSY! WE ARE BUSY PEOPLE.
It seems that in our family, there was always some activity going on or some sporting event that one of the kids was participating in. During the school year, kids are involved in all manner of activities. And the end of the school year is no exception. From graduations, church and school banquets, to weddings, is there ever a free moment? Does this sound like your family?

As we have grown older and our kids are out of the house, it still seems that there is plenty to be stressed out about. But, if I stress out, I can cause a real "fuss" in my household. The only other alternative is to be still and let God be in control. I choose the latter. I realize that I am not the only one with a busy schedule. I know that most are equally as busy as I am, if not busier. Many of you are not only wives and mothers, but you work full-time jobs as well. I admire you for keeping it all together.

Even though the school year is busy, when it starts to come to a close, look ahead to your summer and begin to plan so you will not look back in retrospect wishing that you had done something differently. Summer time can often be a slower paced few months, and it is a great time to capitalize on getting things done and getting your life put in order. As Scripture tells us, "life is but a vapor," and we must make the most of each day that God gives to us. If you have not noticed by now, organization plays such a key role in every single aspect of life. I trust some of these thoughts will be a help to you as you begin to prepare for the next summer that arrives. Please take note of the following.

- Take out that calendar and have a plan of attack.

- Children and adults need a schedule, even in the summer time.

- Keep your time with the Lord as a top priority. Don't allow the summer months to take you away from the most important area of your life.

- Assign duties and responsibilities for your children. They do not need to play all day, every day. Every day of summer is not a holiday.

- Plan time away with your family. These are important times for you to bond with your children and husband.

- Plan your vacation time so that you do not miss out on important church events such as a youth conference or an anniversary Sunday.

- If your house is not in order, take some time to get it organized before the children are out of school.

- Try to plan special "alone" time with each of your children. These are precious memories, and this time allows you to find out what is going on in the life of your child. You might be surprised what you don't know!

- As much as you can, plan something special each week for your family to do together.

- Seek the counsel of someone older and wiser than you for areas where you need help. Don't be too proud to ask when you need it.

- Look forward to each day with anticipation. Please don't endure the summer months; instead, enjoy them.

- Remember that school always resumes the first week of September, and you will regain your peace and sanity.

▸ Help your children find ways to serve during the summer.

It is my prayer, every year, that when school resumes in the fall, we will all be able to look back on the summer with delight instead of regret.

*Trust in the LORD with all thine heart; and lean
not unto thine own understanding.*

—PROVERBS 3:5

CHAPTER SIX

Accepting Change

I DON'T KNOW ABOUT YOU, BUT I AM A nester by nature; I really like things to stay pretty much the same. However, change is inevitable for all of us, and we need to learn to accept it for what it is.

Becoming a grandparent was a big change for my husband and me. Our first grandson, Titus, entered the world two days before Pastors' Conference in 2004. Since my son-in-law was the conference coordinator, I, Nana, was left in charge for a few days. Titus is a joy to our family and is very laid back and easygoing—which is not typical of either Dad or Papa! But, this time was definitely a great change.

The second big change in our lives came with the marriage of our youngest daughter, Tabitha, to Chris

Fanara. Weddings, of course, take time (not to mention money); and they can really send us women on quite the emotional roller coaster! Being left in the house with two men caused me to realize that this was a change I really needed to embrace. I had to work on getting over the "nest-empty-of-girls syndrome" that I experienced. Guys aren't really all bad! After all, I gained a son; I didn't lose a daughter, right?

Another important change in our household was when our son, Tim, graduated from Golden State Baptist College. Tim has always been a delight to us and has brought so much joy as we have watched him grow physically, academically, and spiritually. Since he is our only son, this change was especially hard for me. What did the future hold for him? Where would he end up in the ministry? Would he feel the need to go away to establish his own identity? Time went by so quickly. Just yesterday he was playing T-ball, and now he is a married, a college graduate serving as the youth pastor of the great North Valley Baptist Church. The thought that we really had such little time with him in our home brought on the red eyes and crying stage yet again.

What changes have you experienced this year? Some have had countless trials and struggles, while others have had busy, yet joyous times. Whatever changes you have gone through, ask the Lord to help you to accept each one. God knows exactly what He is doing in our lives. If we rest in the fact that Romans 8:28 is really there for us to claim, we will always come out victorious.

Change? I don't always enjoy it at the time, but it always ends up for my good. Don't fight it. Instead, accept it, and see what God will do for you. Learn to trust the One Who holds your future.

Flee also youthful lusts: but follow righteousness, faith, charity, peace, with them that call on the Lord out of a pure heart.

—II Timothy 2:22

CHAPTER SEVEN

On Rearing Teens

IT HAS BEEN THE THRILL OF A LIFETIME to watch my three children grow up and marry, then to witness them serving the Lord in His harvest field. I am looking forward with great anticipation to all that God has for our family as we serve Him together at the great North Valley Baptist Church in Santa Clara, California—our assigned mission field. I have become ever more aware of the truth I have known, that North Valley is certainly an Acts 1:8 church, taking the Gospel to every creature.

One of the highlights of our year and first major event of our church's summer is the Western National Youth Conference. What a privilege it is each year to minister to our teens and to teenagers from churches across the nation. So many of you have children who are in the midst of those teen years. Enjoy them! Don't grumble and complain about every activity and sporting event. Teenagers are not aliens from another planet; although you will at times be convinced they are in a "different world." If you have teens in your home, please ponder these tips for raising a godly teen. Enjoy this journey with them. The time will be gone before you can blink your eyes.

. . .

Encourage

Encourage your teenager in the things of Christ. Speaking of spiritual matters should not be foreign in your home. The most important factor in your teen's self-image is his relationship with you as a parent.

Pray

Pray for your teenager every day. Each teen should have at least one dedicated page in your prayer journal. There isn't anything too great for God to handle. We cannot be everywhere, see everything, and know everything—but God can. The battle for our teens' lives is waged on our knees. Pray a hedge of protection around your teen. Pray for him in body, soul, and spirit. Pray for the heart of your teen and for your teen to have discernment and desire godly wisdom.

Endear

Endear the heart of your teenager to the pastor, youth pastor, and other spiritual leaders in his life. If your teen cannot shake hands and look these men in the eye, your teen has a problem. Don't pass it off as being "shy."

Support

Pray for your teen's spiritual leaders. Teenagers place so much confidence in them, and those leaders need your prayer support as they guide your teen in paths of righteousness.

Guide

Your teenager should be making many decisions by this time in his life. Be there to guide and direct him, but do not make every decision for him. A person must learn to live with his choices and, yes, sometimes the consequences of those choices.

Live in the Present

Be really careful about using the phrase, "When I was your age." Unless teens ask about your era, be careful not to always be telling them about it. Many things have changed since you were a teen. Do I need to make a list? Do not expect your teen to like all the same things that you like. Remember that your "era" is over.

Lead

Please don't be a "buddy" to your teen. While a parent can be a close friend, a teen really needs you to be the parent! After all, that is your role.

Respect

Respect your teenager. He is a human being with feelings too. Listen more than you lecture. Your teens are in more need of models than critics.

Be Aware

Get your head out of the sand. Be aware of the following: What is my teen wearing? What is my teen watching? What is he reading? What is his favorite music? Pay attention to sudden changes in behavior. After the horrendous massacre at Virginia Tech, it became apparent that there were obvious symptoms prior to this horrible shooting. Know who your teen is. Have your teen spend time at your house rather than at the home of a friend. Watch for warning signs such as spending too much time alone, being withdrawn, and wearing clothing predominantly of one particular color.

Wise Up

Wise is the parent who knows the friends of his teen and the relationships he has in person, and online. Don't assume that all of his friends are good influences. So many are just the opposite. "If any of you lack wisdom, let him ask of God" (James 1:5).

Cherish

Teen years don't last forever. Don't destroy your future adult relationship with your teen due to conflicts during his teen years. Enjoy these years. Your teenager will never pass this way again. Help him to look back with joy instead of regrets.

Be Authentic

Please don't be one person at church and another at home. Believe it or not, teens know when an adult is real. Inconsistency will never produce consistency. Don't expect your teen to display more self control than you do. To bring up a teen in the way he should go, travel that way yourself once in a while. Remember with a teen that "your walk talks louder than your talk talks."

Invest

Stay connected with your teen. That will only happen by spending time with them and knowing how to communicate with them. Communication is a must! Don't give your teen the idea that you are too busy for him. He should be one of your top priorities.

Discipline

Don't make excuses for bad behavior. Discipline is still a major part of rearing a teen. You may need to receive good counsel in this area. Correction should be swift, reasonable, and related to the offense. Don't disapprove of what your teen is—disapprove of what he does.

Keep Private

Do not discuss your teen's personal problems with everybody. He should be able to walk into church without thinking, "Everyone is staring at me!"

Love

Love your teen for who he is. (Parental love is the first love a child experiences and understands.) Teens need love, especially when they don't deserve it.

Require Accountability

Know what kind of music your teen is listening to as well as what video games and videos he is playing and watching. Don't let a teen have a TV in his bedroom. Take control of the computer and internet. You should not allow your teen to have a computer in his bedroom, and you should be the one to log him on. No teen should ever spend time on the internet without adult supervision.

Influence

When you seem to think your teen "thinks he knows it all," remember he doesn't. A teen needs your guidance and wisdom more than ever. Please don't leave the rearing of your teen up to the pastor, youth pastor, principal, and Christian school teachers. You are (or should be) the number one leader and influence in his life.

. . .

My teens are all raised. They are now all married and have children of their own. I do not get to start anew with my teens. Those days are gone and will never return. Enjoy these days because, before too long, you will be ushered down the aisle as the mother of the bride or groom. You will hear the Bridal March, listen to their vows, and watch as they ride off into the sunset, starting their journey called life. Yes, it happens just that quickly. Enjoy!

Teens really are awesome! But remember that rules without relationships always breed rebellion. Cultivate that relationship with your teen today while there is time.

Lo, children are an heritage of the LORD: and the fruit of the womb is his reward.

—PSALM 127:3

CHAPTER EIGHT

A Nana and Papa's Heart

OVER THE YEARS, THE TRIEBER FAMILY HAS "blossomed" with the addition of our grandchildren. The old cliché, "If I had known grandchildren were so much fun, I would have had them first" is definitely true for my husband and me. We are definitely enjoying our children's children. I realize that I have not been a Nana for as long as some, but I would like to share some of the things I have learned from being a grandparent over the years. I trust that it might be a blessing to you.

- Pray for your grandchildren every day. Start the minute you find out the good news.
- As difficult as it is, do not give unsought advice.

- Pray for your daughter or daughter-in-law as she carries the baby. She will need health, strength, and extra rest at this time.

- Buy something for the "expected" child and the mother to show your excitement!

- Do little things for the expectant mother during the nine months.

- Begin your baby room/corner in your home. A nana should always have diapers, bottles and formula, toys, and goodies at her house.

- Write down special stories and memories that you will want to share with this new little one. Our granddaughter loves to hear stories about her mommy, her auntie, and uncle when they were little. We have told the same story many a time.

- Learn how to take pictures! I always need help in this area.

- Start a baby book for each grandchild. You will have the most in the first grandchild's book if you do not work at it with each one.

- Enjoy every minute of being a grandparent. It is so much fun. You can love and spoil those grandchildren then send them home!

Enjoy every moment of time with your family. Create a fun atmosphere for your family, and remember that life is what you make it.

He hath made his wonderful works to be remembered: the LORD is gracious and full of compassion.

—PSALM III:4

CHAPTER NINE

Precious Memories

"WE DON'T REMEMBER DAYS, WE REMEMBER moments" is the quote stenciled on one of the walls in our home that I call my memory wall. As I am sure it is for you, family is so important to us. Creating memories with our family is what will last us a lifetime. I can remember our family when I was growing up and what memories we can share when all eight of us Swanson kids are together. Precious memories flood my soul as I think back on those good times.

Often, my house seems so quiet, and I am very reminiscent about days gone by—days that had once been filled with the sounds of raising children. But, not content to succumb to quietness, my husband and I often fill up the hours with bike rides, walks, coffee and tea times around the fire pit in the backyard, and countless hours of family time with the whole gang. We have had cookouts, campouts, birthday parties, game nights, rides, dinners, friends over, and many special times together. Our home has always been a place of comfort for our children. It is a place where we can kick off our shoes and let down our hair. It's a place of transparency and vulnerability; a place where we are completely known yet completely loved. It is truly a place called home. Decorations for every season will be in place a month or so ahead of time, and it seems as if our schedules are always in full swing. Every season of the year and every season of life has so much to offer us.

As I yield every day to the Holy Spirit and as I stay connected to Jesus Christ, I stay connected with my family and those I love in a way that is both rewarding and delightful. My relationship to Jesus Christ must stay solid and secure, for then and only then am I really able to enjoy every season of life.

I trust that your family's memories have been as wonderful as mine. If they have not, ask the Lord to help you in the next season of the year, to make it one of the most unforgettable seasons for you and your loved ones.

Thy word is a lamp unto my feet, and a light unto my path.

—Psalm 119:105

CHAPTER TEN

The Value of a Marked Bible

ONE SUMMER, PASTOR, TIM AND I HAD THE wonderful privilege to go to Rockford, Illinois, my home place, to enjoy the anniversary of the Berean Baptist Church and my dad's anniversary of being the pastor. I enjoyed seeing all of my brothers and their families. My sister, Vennie, and her family were able to accompany us on the trip as well. All eight members of the Swanson clan were together at one time! We were able to have the Memorial Day picnic on the family farm. I will admit that I was quite envious of all the acres of green grass that my brothers' grandchildren are able to enjoy with their tractors, trucks and the like! Someone once said, "The grass may be greener, but you just have to mow it." That may be true, but you can only "hose off" concrete.

One of the greatest events of this trip was a special presentation that Dad had for me on Friday night prior to our flying home. I have been literally begging my dad for one of his many Bibles for years, but to no avail. On that special evening, Dad gave me one of his Bibles. In addition, my brother, DeWayne, gave me the only Bible we have from my mom, who passed away in 1970. What tears of joy I shed! I cannot begin to tell you how much I have enjoyed reading through these Bibles. To see markings in their own handwriting has been thrilling.

My dad is an ardent student of the Word of God and is phenomenal in his knowledge of the Bible. Page after page of his Bible is filled with notes and sermons! He commented to me that this Bible wasn't "marked up" like some of his other Bibles, but I can't begin to tell you how "marked up" this one is. I have found many "ladies' sermons" in the pages of his Bible which I intend to use. (Sorry, Dad, I know they are copyrighted!)

I have equally enjoyed reading through Mom's Bible; I hold it as one of my most cherished earthly possessions. Both of these precious treasures now grace my coffee table for my children and grandchildren to hold and look through.

Most of us have more than one Bible. I have several Bibles that I have kept down through the years. It is my prayer that my children will cherish one of Mom's "marked" Bibles as much as I have enjoyed these two special Bibles. With that in mind, let me ask you a few questions:

▸ Are you marking a Bible for your children?

▸ Is your Bible available for your children to see?

▸ Do your children catch you reading your Bible?

▸ How much time do you actually spend in your Bible?

▸ Is it evident in your daily life that you read the Bible?

. . .

If you cannot answer a resounding "yes" to these questions, why not get started today? The song writer so aptly penned, "The B-I-B-L-E, yes, that's the Book for me. I stand alone on the Word of God, the B-I-B-L-E."

If you are marking your Bible, there is no doubt that it will, in turn, mark you.

Let all things be done decently and in order.

—I CORINTHIANS 14:40

CHAPTER ELEVEN

A Life of Order

AS I THRIVE ON MAKING OUR HOME A special place and an oasis for my family, I try to always stay ahead of the game and get the house decorated for the upcoming season. Nearing the end of the summer, I have already decorated our house for the fall season. Potpourri is simmering on the stove and a combination of white and orange lights are intertwined with garland over the windows, doors, fireplace, and banisters. Fall decorations are everywhere at the Trieber house.

Structure is so vitally important to a family. Homes shouldn't still be getting into a routine and schedule for school in October or November. When the long days of summer are coming to an end, it is time to start planning and preparing your home for the fall schedule. Dear lady, you are the one responsible for guiding the home. So much depends on you. Children need a schedule and a home of order. This is designed by our Lord in Scripture when He instructs us to do all things "decently and in order" (I Corinthians 14:40). A home filled with chaos will likely create a dysfunctional family. Yet, it seems that homes in America these days are out of control! The television, internet, cell phones, iPods, and other wonderful devices are taking the place of family fun and the ability to have a downright good time together. Please, don't let this happen to your family. I trust that the following suggestions might be helpful to you.

Clean House

Clear out clutter. Once your children are in school, go through the house and de-clutter. Don't hoard unnecessary or unused items!

Create a Calendar

Mark your calendar, your control center, and keep it out where you can actually see it. I always suggest the kitchen being your calendar center since that is the most convenient place to allow everyone in the family to see what's going on.

Plan Meals

Have a meal planner. Take a few minutes each week to

plan the menu for the next week. Nutrition is of utmost importance to the health of our children. Childhood diseases are at an all time high in America. McDonald's just won't cut it. Please spend time in the kitchen. Eat good food and eat regularly. Skipping meals is not healthy.

Drink Water

Help your family to drink plenty of water. Stay away from caffeine and junk food. They rob your body of important nutrients.

Eliminate Laundry

Keep up with laundry. Don't let it pile up! Remember: wash, dry, fold, and put it away instead of letting it sit around the house.

Designate Family Chores

Teach family members to do chores. It will not kill them to help out around the house.

Organize Toys

Have a place for children's toys. Use baskets, bins, and shelves to get all of their activity items in one place. You do not need toys in every room of the house. Teach your children where their belongings go, and make them learn early on to put them away after using them.

Put Things in Place

Have a place for everything, and put everything in its place. Never go to bed when the house is a mess. Take a few minutes to pick up before heading off to bed. You will be so glad you did the next morning! Remember the rule: "Don't put it down; put it away."

Decorate Your Home

Take time to make your home cozy, warm, and inviting. Michael's, Target, T.J. Maxx, and Big Lots all have wonderful fall decorations available. Start with a few, and add to them each year.

Meet with God

Have a place in your home where you meet with the Lord on a daily basis. Your Bible, prayer lists, and study guides should be included in this special place. Please take time to meet with the Lord. Our husbands, children, church, and country are so desperately in need of our prayers. If we don't pray, who will? Talk to God as you pillow your head. He will carry your burdens and concerns through the night.

Plan Time with Children

Plan special quiet times with each child during the day. Don't let them think that everything else is more important than they are.

Make Time with Your Husband

And don't forget number one—your husband! Husbands and wives need time at the end of each day to discuss the day's happenings and reconnect with each other. It is so easy to put the children first, but don't do so at the expense of your relationship with your spouse. Your children will one day leave the house, but you will still have your husband after they are long gone.

Secure Time for Yourself

Take a good walk or do some form of exercise every day. Include time for a nap if you need it. Your family will be thankful you did. Take a bubble bath and relax before you crawl into bed. Light a candle just because you enjoy it. Don't feel guilty about taking time for yourself; it will, in turn, help you to take better care of your family.

Plan for Tomorrow

Plan for the next day before you go to bed. Make a to do list and stick to it! Set the table for breakfast before you go to bed.

Arrange Family Devotions

Encourage your husband in family devotions, and create a godly atmosphere in the home. A cozy, warm house without spirituality will not help when the storms of life are crashing upon you.

WITH ALL MY HEART

Create a Peaceful Home

Quiet down your house early in the evening and create an atmosphere conducive to a good night's sleep. Sleep is so important to the health of your family.

Try Again

Never give up! Every new month, each new week, and a brand new day tomorrow grants each one of us a chance to try again. If you feel as though you have tried and failed, please remember my favorite cliché: "Cry a river, build a bridge, and get over it!"

Tips for a Good School Year

While we are in the structure zone, here are some ideas our family has used for getting organized and into a new school year. I practiced what I am suggesting to you to help me with all three of my children from K-5 through their college years. I trust that these thoughts will be a help to you and your family.

Prioritize Events

Set your school schedule. Get a calendar out, and get organized. Make sure to write down all of the special events that are going to take place.

Stock Up

Rather than wait until someone needs something for school, have a few items in stock so you don't end up running yourself crazy by trying to shop the night before an item is needed. Get your school supply shopping done as early as possible.

Stay on Schedule

Make sure that your children are on a good schedule, and stick to it. Children need to be in bed at a decent hour. Too many of our children and teenagers are staying up way too late at night. It shows up the next day at school.

Plan Lunches

Decide which days your children are going to purchase a hot lunch and which days they will be bringing a lunch. Hot lunch does cost money, so set aside a little each week.

Pray

Spend time in prayer for your children. With the beginning of school, they have plenty on their plates too. Be extra careful to treat them with love and care. Remember that you are not the only one going through a transition.

Praise

Look at the school year with a positive attitude. Don't get caught up in being negative about teachers, money, busyness, etc. Praise will take care of the negative.

Meet with Teachers

Meet your children's teachers early on in the year. Write them a note and be sure that you have added their name(s) to your prayer list.

Enjoy the Grade

Enjoy this school year. Your child will, hopefully, never be in this grade again.

Take Charge

Be in charge of your child's life. Too many parents leave everything up to the Christian school. You're the parent so why not act like one?

Have a great school year. It will be what you make it!

She will do him good and not evil all the days of her life.

—PROVERBS 31:12

CHAPTER TWELVE

A Wife's Role

ONE OF THE GREATEST OPPORTUNITIES given me was to teach a class on "The Home" with my husband, Bro. Trieber, at Golden State Baptist College. We were privileged to have between 140 and 150 students in this class. Needless to say, we had a great time. Most enjoyable for me was the question-and-answer time allotted at the end of each class hour. Our college students had serious and sincere concerns regarding marriage and the home. As I glanced over the classroom, I did not just see a "sea of faces." Instead, I saw our future. It was a sobering thought to remember that the Christian leaders of tomorrow are sitting in classrooms today.

One of my utmost concerns as a wife, mother, nana, and pastor's wife is the responsibility I have to train the wonderful young ladies the Lord brings to our campus to be godly wives and mothers. Our nation is in a world of hurt and depends on Christian women to take seriously these important roles given to us by God. As I study Scripture, especially in Proverbs, Ephesians, and Titus, I find quite a list of responsibilities I must accept in order to fulfill my role of "wife" to my husband. The following is an excerpt from my prayer journal; it is my prayer that my list will inspire you to do the same for your husband. My list of "musts" is as follows:

- I must help him.

- I must submit to him. *(Ouch! I said it!)*

- I must obey him.

- I must be desirable to him. *(Take a look in the mirror!)*

- I must love him.

- I must be virtuous.

- I must do him good.

- I must be frugal.

- I must be balanced.

- I must control my tongue.

- I must be a keeper at home.

- I must have children that respect me.

- I must fear the Lord.
- I must guide my home in the direction my husband has set.
- I must maintain a good testimony.
- I must keep his confidence.
- I must be discreet.
- I must be chaste.
- I must be domestic.
- I must be loving and affectionate.

Let me encourage you to create your own list of "musts" as you study the Scriptures. Remember that each one of us is an example for others to follow, and "may all who come behind us find us faithful."

She is not afraid of the snow for her household:
for all her household are clothed with scarlet.

—PROVERBS 31:21

CHAPTER THIRTEEN

Making Your House a Home

BACK IN 2009, I HAD THE JOY OF TRAVELING (by American Airlines, which is major for those of you who know me) with my sister, Vennie, her daughter Jennifer and her son Austin (my niece and nephew), and my dear friend of many years, Pat Carr. Jennifer and Pat were able to stay only a short time, but we made so many memories together that we will not forget for a lifetime.

We did a lot of sightseeing and reminiscing to say the least. It was such a beautiful time of year, and the fall colors were breathtaking. I took Pat by all of the places from my childhood, and she very quickly became our full-time photographer. I took her to the family farm, the old Berean Baptist Church where I met and married Bro. Trieber, the houses that I once lived in as a kid, the high school from which I graduated, the cemetery where my mom is laid to rest, and a place very dear to my heart—3130 Blackstone Avenue, the house where I got saved. It was such fun to be with my six brothers, my sister, and my dad. My family surprised me with a birthday party while we were there. I had not celebrated a birthday with my family in 35 years! Also, upon Pat's request, our family gathered at my brother's house on Wednesday night after church for a family singspiration! I enjoyed watching as my dear dad held the songbook in his hand and sang with tears flowing down his cheeks! It had to be a joy for him to witness all of his children singing hymns together around the piano.

One of the most thrilling events for me was being able to go out to the Edwards Apple Orchard and take pictures with all eight of us kids and Dad. That was a time I will hold dear to my heart forever. To sum that photo session up—my brothers are crazy!

My sister and I were able to spend precious times just talking with our dad. What an amazing man! We were able to look through many of his study materials from pastoring the Berean Baptist Church for over 50 years, and that was a very moving time for both my sister and me. The Friday night before we flew out, he gave us both a few of his study notebooks for our sons. He gave me a special Bible study book of his for our son,

Melvin and Geraldine Swanson

Our Wedding Day - December 23, 1972

Pastor and Mrs. Trieber - 1977

The Trieber Family - 1982

Tiffany - 1982

Tim - 1984

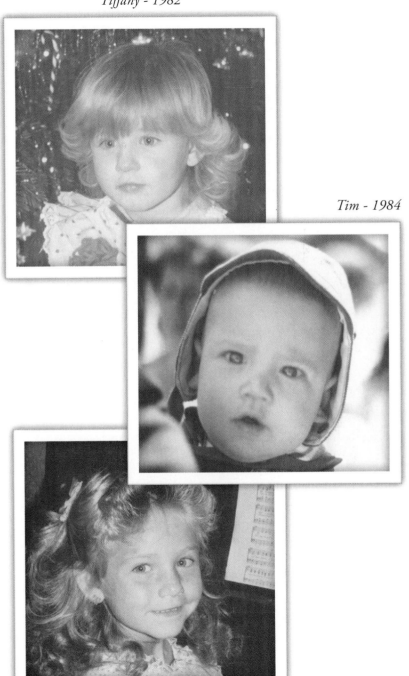

Tabitha - 1988

Church Banquet - 1975

Parent-Baby Dedication - 1984

The Trieber Kids

First Day of School - 1990

Anniversary Sunday - 1988

A Day at Church - 1998

North Valley Baptist School Homecoming

Tiffany and Ryan - 1994

Family Vacation - 1996

Tim and Tabitha with Mom

Tim's Wedding - 2009

Titus, Tim, and TJ

Me and My Girls

Nana and Papa with a Few of the Grandkids

Rhegan Fanara - January 2010

Riley, Titus, Ashlyn, TJ

The Fanara Family

The Thompson Family

The Trieber Family

The Whole Family

My Parents' Bibles

My Sister and Brothers

My Husband and Me

Tim. I had fun staking my claim on several things that I want of his, but, having six brothers back there might be a problem! I will have to plan a trip unbeknownst to them to claim my treasures. We were all arguing over one particular picture of the family farm that hangs in Dad's living room. I am sure that, being his favorite child, the picture will be mine.

We took a ride through beautiful Page Park which is just across the street from the church. How I remember so many activities in that place. I remember when school was cancelled because of snow, Dad would take us there to make snow angels and go sledding down the little hills—which, back then, I thought were the biggest hills ever! The things we remember through the eyes of a child.

My trip back home to Illinois was such a special memory. I am so grateful for the upbringing that I had. We didn't have a lot of things but we did a lot of things together.

My mom and dad dearly loved each other. Many times when Mom was folding Dad's laundry, she would say, "I love the man that wears these clothes!" Back then, I thought, "Thanks for sharing, Mom." Now, I say, "Thank you, Mom, for loving my dad."

Mom was actively involved in my dad's ministry. She helped him birth the great Berean Baptist Church. My mom did not have her own agenda. Dad was her only agenda.

Dad played with us kids. As a kid, I remember playing baseball and basketball, sledding, riding on the tractor, and doing many other kinds of activities. Dad was there for us. Work was never more important than we were. Men often don't realize how important they are to their children. The importance of a father's influence can never be underestimated. How he relates to his children will shape their lives for the bad or for the good.

. . .

Let me share some things with you from my upbringing that might be an encouragement and a help for both your marriage and turning your house into a home.

My mom gave of herself unselfishly to her children. I never remember a time when Mom wasn't around.

We had a spiritual home. We were never able to leave the house in the morning before we had family devotions. Back then, I used to think, "Hurry up and get this over with!" Now I say, "Could we take more time for this?"

We were all involved in church. If we weren't at a church service, we were "playing church" someplace in the house.

Dad practiced what he preached. He was not one person to his congregation and another person to his children.

We learned how to work. We could never go anywhere on Saturdays unless the house was cleaned from top to bottom!

We learned that sorrow draws you to the Savior. Everyone experiences loss. It's the part we don't like and wish we never had to go through. But we all will. The death of my mom was the hardest thing I have ever had to go through in my life. It has taught me so much. When someone experiences the loss of a parent, I can truly relate to that person.

We had to get a job in high school. Dad was "old school" enough to make us earn money for what we wanted and, in so doing, he helped us to appreciate what we had more than we would have otherwise.

My parents were balanced. They didn't have "goofy" ideas, and we didn't have a list of rules a mile long. By the way, all of his children are in church every Sunday.

We learned to pray. I witnessed Mom and Dad praying separately and together many times, and we prayed as a family.

We learned loyalty to family. We would often tease each other, but if someone else ever wanted to fight one of us, we all jumped in to rescue our sibling.

We learned about faith. As I heard salvation testimonies of my siblings, it was amazing how many of us were saved at home. What a memory!

We learned how to love. Children cannot live without love. Learn to say "I love you," and say it often.

When your children drive by the places from their childhood and reflect back on their memories as a child, I trust that they too can make a list of their own as I have done. God bless you as you raise your children for His glory, and may He help you to make your marriage and home a little bit of heaven on earth.

Making the Most of Your Holiday Season

One important part of making your house a home is making holiday seasons special. I want to give you a few suggestions that I hope will take some of the frenzy out of the holidays for you and your family. Take time to sit down and plan for the holidays before you find yourself overwhelmed and frustrated when the holidays arrive.

Budget

Plan a budget for holiday spending and stick to it. We always spend too much if we don't plan.

Menu

If you are hosting one of the holidays at your house, plan your menu; buy what you can purchase in advance. Leave your "list" out where you can see it.

Lists

Make your gift list. I suggest that you purchase 3x5 cards. Place the name of each individual for whom you are buying on a separate card. Write sizes and "wants" on each card. After you have purchased the gift or gifts for an individual, staple the receipts on the card and file all the cards in a file box. It will make returns so much easier should they be necessary.

Gift Cards

The older your children get, the harder they are to buy for. Gift cards work great for that "picky" teenager. What teenager doesn't like to do his own shopping?

Thoughtfulness

Try to buy things that people will use. Put some thought into your purchases, and don't shop with an "if they don't like it, they can return it" attitude. People always appreciate gifts that are bought with thoughtfulness.

Memories
Plan to spend time with your family during the holidays. Taking rides to look at Christmas lights, shopping as a family, and of course, that once-a-year family picture are all a few of our favorites.

Order
Take extra care to make sure that your home is in order. It is less stressful if you live by the "don't put it down, put it away" rule. As busy wives and mothers, a messy house only adds to our list of things to do.

Preparation
Buy your Christmas cards early, start addressing them, and get them in the mail.

Time
Enjoy some special baking time with your daughters. This is the time to teach them to bake. It will be a memory they will treasure.

Giving
Remember that "Jesus is the reason for the season." Plan

a special gift that your family can give your church. It could be a monetary gift or something the church specifically needs.

. . .

Planning now for the holidays will make them so much easier for you and so much more enjoyable for everyone. The holidays come at the same time every year, so don't make excuses for your lack of preparation. Have a great time with your family. You will travel this way only once.

But Mary kept all these things, and pondered them in her heart.

—LUKE 2:19

CHAPTER FOURTEEN

Ponder Them in Your Heart

FALL AND WINTER ARE, BY FAR, MY TWO favorite seasons of the year. I always enjoy the cooler, crisp weather (well, for California), and I certainly enjoy decorating the house for Christmas. Christmas music in our home usually begins playing in October, and the white lights of the season are in every room of the house. Every year when I take down the decorations and pack them away, I pray this prayer: "Lord, please let me live to put these decorations out again next year, and may I please enjoy this season again with my family?" Thus far, obviously, those prayers have been answered.

As I ponder my favorite season, the Christmas season, so many memories flood my mind. Having grown up in the Midwest, I can remember ice skating, snowball fights, making snow angels, and so many other activities that I enjoyed as a child. One of my favorite memories is the reading of the Christmas story in Luke chapter two at Christmastime. We were not allowed to open one present in the Swanson family until Dad had read the Christmas story. When the Lord gave my husband and me the privilege of having children, one particular verse took on new meaning for me. This verse is found in Luke 2:19: "But Mary kept all these things, and pondered them in her heart." Mary, as the mother of the Lord Jesus, has a place in history higher than any woman has or will ever have known.

The Bible says that Mary was "blessed among women" (Luke 1:28). Mary is the subject of majestic poems, novels, and plays. She is depicted all over the world on canvas and stained glassed windows, and in bronze, marble, and stone. Mary's greatness had a humble beginning. She was an obscure peasant girl living in Nazareth centuries ago. Her story has spread to the ends of the earth. Though she never entered a palace, her picture has graced the most magnificent of palaces. She never traveled any farther than from Palestine to Egypt, yet her story still travels to the farthest corners of the earth. It had to be a marvel for Mary to carry within her very being the Christ child, who was born to die for the sins of the world. I would enjoy a conversation with

Mary, wouldn't you? I would have a hundred or more questions for her: "What was it like carrying the Lord Jesus? Did you experience morning sickness? What was it like having Him in your home? What was it like to watch your son die on the cross?"

If you are like me, you cannot help but wonder these same questions. One thing that every mother has in common is just that: We are mothers. No man has ever had the awesome privilege of carrying a child and giving birth. (I know, they tell us it is harder on them than on us!) What a blessing and responsibility is placed upon us as mothers. Wise is the mother who learns to keep all these things, and ponder them in her heart concerning her children. We certainly do not need to "share" happenings and incidents in the lives of our children that might cause them humiliation and embarrassment. Equally as wise is the mother who ponders and prays for her children. The world has such a pull for our children. The devil certainly isn't happy when he sees our children turn out to serve the Lord. I pray every day for my own children in these areas:

▸ for their daily health, safety and protection

▸ for purity of mind, soul and body

▸ that they will make wise decisions based on God's word

- for their future and for them to be in God's will
- for the spouses of my married children
- for their children (How could a nana not pray for her grandchildren?)
- that they will be faithful to the house of God
- that they will be led by the Holy Spirit
- for wisdom in financial matters
- that they will grow every day in God's grace

· · ·

This list is certainly not exhaustive; I have many more areas about which I pray for each one of my children. I know that you do too. Our children's safety every day could very well depend upon our prayers. I don't believe that Mary, the mother of the Lord Jesus, was wrapped up in herself; instead, I believe she was consumed with the divine responsibility she was given. It is my prayer that we, as mothers, will keep all these things, and ponder them in our hearts.

Whereas ye know not what shall be on the morrow. For what is your life? It is even a vapour, that appeareth for a little time, and then vanisheth away.

—JAMES 4:14

CHAPTER FIFTEEN

Value of Time

HAVE YOU EVER ASKED YOURSELF, "WHAT could I do if I just had more time?" It seems like there is never enough time!

So often, I have been in the "hustle and bustle" of life, including getting to travel and speak at conferences. I have often caught myself saying, "In no way am I ready to head out of town." I always have too much to do before I go.

Webster's dictionary defines time as "every moment there has ever been or ever will be." It also lists several other definitions. In fact, the list was quite long compared to other words, indicating to me that time is something not to be taken for granted.

Often I have commented, "That was a waste of time," or "I didn't have time to get that done," and so on. I certainly would not want my time on earth to come to an abrupt end and leave my family and friends with the thought that I never had time for them. We are never going to have more hours in our day or more days in the week or month. We only have so much time. If time is so valuable, how can we be more effective with the time we do have? I am glad you asked. The following has been of help to me, and maybe it will be to you too.

- Write down all yearly events on your calendar.

- Plan for the week ahead on the Friday before.

- Start every day with God. Have a time, a place, and a plan.

- Include others in your schedule. Take time for soul winning and reaching out to others. Be sure you are living right. You can't give what you don't have.

- Do special things for the special people in your life.

- Never leave the presence of your loved ones without telling them that you love them.

- Organize your home. A house out of order is a life out of order.

▸ Don't waste time watching television. There is no "delete" button on the mind, so be careful what you put into it.

▸ Live your life by a schedule.

• • •

Live every day as though it were your last. A few years ago, my brother, DeWayne, was admitted to the hospital with congestive heart failure. Little did he know when his day started that he would end up in the hospital. I am glad that in the days prior to his being admitted to the hospital I had been calling him, telling him that I love him, and was praying for him. We never know what tomorrow holds, but we know Who holds tomorrow.

Time is precious. As the Bible says, our lives are but vapors. This day is the tomorrow we planned for yesterday. Make the most of each day—start today!

The heart of her husband doth safely trust in her,
so that he shall have no need of spoil.

—PROVERBS 31:11

CHAPTER SIXTEEN

A Happy Home

IT SEEMS THAT IN THIS DAY WE LIVE IN, we have forgotten the core elements that make a good home. We must get back to the basics! Here are some ideas that were commonly taught in the 1950s to help young girls prepare to be wives and mothers.

Have Dinner Ready

Plan ahead, even the night before, to have a delicious meal—on time. This is a way of letting your husband know you have been thinking about him, and are concerned about his needs. Most men are hungry when they come home and the prospects of a good meal are part of the warm welcome needed.

Prepare Yourself

Take a few minutes to rest so you will be refreshed when he arrives. Touch up your make-up, your hair, and look fresh. He has just been with a lot of work-weary people. Be happy and a little more interesting. His boring day may need a lift.

Clear Away Clutter

Make one last trip through the main part of the house just before your husband arrives, gathering up school books, toys, paper, etc. Then run a dust cloth over the tables. Your husband will feel he has reached a haven of rest and order, and it will give you a lift too.

Prepare the Children

Take a few minutes to wash the children's hands and faces if they are small, comb their hair, and, if necessary, change their clothes. They are little treasures, and he would like to see them playing the part.

Make Him Comfortable

Have him lean back in a comfortable chair or suggest he lie down in the bedroom. Have a cool or warm drink ready for him. Arrange his pillow and offer to take off his shoes. Speak in a low, soft, soothing and pleasant voice. Allow him to relax and unwind.

Minimize the Noise

At the time of his arrival, eliminate all noise of the washer, dryer, or vacuum. Greet him with a warm smile and be glad to see him.

Don't Complain

Don't greet him with problems or complaints. Don't complain at the dinner table. Count this as minor compared with what he might have gone through that day.

Listen to Him

You may have a dozen things to tell him, but the moment of his arrival is not the time. Let him talk first.

Make the Evening His

Never complain if he does not take you out to dinner or other places of entertainment; instead, try to understand his world of strain and pressure and his need to be home and relax.

The Goal

Make your home a place of peace and order where your husband can relax.

When pondering these instructions of yesteryear, it is plain to see that we have come a long way in our homes, but in the wrong direction. Let us return to Biblical, loving homes, where each member lives a life of selfless service for the others in the family.

For this child I prayed; and the LORD *hath given me my petition which I asked of him.*

—I SAMUEL 1:27

CHAPTER SEVENTEEN

∽

What Every Mother Should Know

WE LIVE IN A DAY WHEN THE POSITIONS of wives, husbands, and parents are under attack. Bro. Trieber and I have never taken our role as parents lightly. I would venture to say that one of the reasons is we were married for a few years before the Lord gave us our first child, Tiffany. I remember attending other ladies' baby showers while thinking, "Is this ever going to happen to me?" I prayed every day that God would give us a baby; and in His time, not mine, He did. My own experience is why the story of Hannah in the book of I Samuel is one of my favorite Bible stories. Hannah prayed fervently for a child. To me, Hannah is the woman who personifies the ideal mother in the Old Testament. Hannah was the mother of Samuel, the earliest of the great Hebrew prophets after Moses and the last of the judges. Samuel was the "worthy son of a worthy mother." Before she had Samuel, Hannah left her home in Ramah each year to go to the temple at Shiloh where her most ardent prayer was for a child. God answered her prayer and gave her Samuel. I claimed I Samuel 1:27 while I was expecting Tiffany: "For this child I prayed; and the LORD hath given me my petition which I asked of him." I also learned the following from studying the life of Hannah, and I would like to share it with you.

1. Hannah's Prayer

- She prayed with fervency. Hannah prayed again and again. When she undoubtedly felt like quitting, she prayed again.

- She was a woman who prayed in the good times and in the bad.

- Hannah walked close to the Lord. It isn't enough to walk close to the Lord when times are good; we must walk even closer when times are bad.

All of us have undoubtedly gone through experiences that have caused us devastating pain. Hannah's pain was because she didn't have a child. Keep in mind that no life is filled with so much pain that the God of all comfort cannot reach down with a healing touch. He did for Hannah, and her touch was a little baby boy she could hold in her arms.

2. Hannah's Provision

- She received a man child from God. I received my first child, Tiffany; three years later, Tim was born; and 13 months after the birth of Tim, the Lord blessed us with Tabitha. (I then prayed that He would stop!)

- Because Hannah walked in God's will, she was in a place of safety. Walking in the will of God brings safety to me as well as to my children. I would rather have my children on the mission field in God's will than here in Santa Clara, out of God's will.

- Hannah stayed connected to the one who planned her destiny. If we do not stay connected, we can sell out in one moment of weakness.

3. Hannah's Praise

- She praised the Lord for answered prayer. Don't quit praying. You might be closer to the answer than you think.

‣ She was able to praise the Lord because she gave Samuel back to God. Samuel was able to serve in the temple.

‣ Having children turn out for the Lord brings praise; but, at the same time, I realize having children who live for God is all because of His grace.

. . .

I praise the Lord for the husband, children, sons-in-law, daughter-in-law, and grandchildren that He has given me, but please don't think having a family that serves the Lord came to pass without fervency in prayer.

Everyone's needs are different. However, I once heard our missionary, Bro. Tommy Ashcraft, pray this prayer; and I have used it time and time again: "If you need correction, I pray you will receive it. If you need comfort, I pray that God will be the God of all comfort to you. If you need changing, I pray that God will change you."

That is my prayer for you. Is anything too hard for the Lord? You do not have one problem that is beyond His power to solve! Ask Him today.

Therefore shall a man leave his father and his mother, and shall cleave unto his wife: and they shall be one flesh.

—Genesis 2:24

CHAPTER EIGHTEEN

———— ∽ ————

Letting Them Go

I DON'T THINK MY CHILDREN WOULD disagree with me when I say that I sincerely try to be a great mother-in-law. When your child chooses a life's partner in marriage, it is very important that you accept and love that person for who he or she is.

As our family enlarged itself, our love enlarged as well to encompass those that have joined our family. We have a long list of folks in our church who are adding married children to their family. This is one of the benefits and blessings of having stayed at North Valley for so many years. Watching our church kids grow up and marry is both rewarding and fulfilling as a pastor's wife.

I am confident that I am not the perfect mother-in-law, and I have been the brunt of many a mother-in-law joke; but, I try to put into practice the following which I will share with you. When your children marry:

Let them be themselves. Don't try to make them a carbon copy of you!

Don't enforce your rules on them. God will speak to them as He does you.

Treat each one special. The old cliché "blood is thicker than water" should not apply to your sons- and daughters-in-law.

Encourage them. Let them know you are proud of what they are becoming through Christ.

Do special things for them. Money is, more often than not, scarce in those early days. I know that, with the economy right now, we all could use a little extra. But if you can be a blessing financially, do so. Don't have that "great depression attitude" of, "We didn't have it when we were their age." Life isn't the same as when you grew up.

Keep your opinions to yourself. Unless you are asked or you are all involved in a discussion, don't speak your mind.

Allow your sons-in-law to be the head of their families. Ouch! I can't believe I said that. If I had the time, I would share with you how my son-in-law Ryan made that very clear to me early on in his marriage to our oldest daughter. I can remember the time, and I can show you the place.

Don't expect them to do everything just like you do it. Your daughters might set up housekeeping differently than you. It's their house, not yours. Let them decorate and arrange their homes as they desire.

Let them include you as they want to. Don't pout if they choose not to. Believe it or not, they will have their own circle of friends.

Enjoy the times you do have with your married children. If you are all that you should be as an in-law, guess what? They all come home and those are extra special times for you.

Enjoy those married children, and think about all of those wonderful grandbabies they will bring into your family. They are worth it!

*The steps of a good man are ordered by the LORD:
and he delighteth in his way.*

—PSALM 37:23

_ოჳ_

Don't Let Crisis Control You

WHEN OUR YOUNGEST DAUGHTER, TABITHA, was hospitalized with preeclampsia in 2006, her situation was really touch and go for several days as doctors tried to determine whether she needed to go ahead and deliver, which would cause our little grandson to be born prematurely. As her situation stabilized, she became a bit antsy about her long stay in the hospital. For any who may know her, she is our very active child and doesn't like to be confined. We had to realize that God had a lesson in that seemingly frustrating situation for each of us, and we certainly had to trust Him for the outcome. She was blessed with a great doctor, a member of our church. She also had wonderful nurses attending to her, and we were able to witness to so many.

On July 4, just a few days after Tabitha was admitted to the hospital, my mother-in-law fell and broke her hip. She was in a great deal of pain until the doctor operated that following night. It was several weeks before she was able to return home since she was admitted to a skilled nursing facility to help her recover better.

All of these events kept me and my husband very busy, traveling back and forth between two hospitals. We were scheduled for a vacation to Hawaii that year and had to set that aside until later. But, we were thankful that we were able to be around when everything took place. I learned many things over those next several weeks that I think might help you if and when you find yourself in a situation similar to the ones I have described above.

• • •

Everyone's world doesn't stop when you have a crisis. Don't expect people to drop everything and come to help you with your problem. God is enough, and He gives unusual grace when you need it.

Live in a way that will allow you to get your prayers answered. I am thankful that I have not had to make phone calls to get right with anyone. I try to live every day with the thought that my family's safety just might depend on my prayers that day.

- Be very thankful for everything and anything that anyone does for you. Those are added blessings not to be taken for granted.

- Live in God's Word, and pray without ceasing.

- When others go through a crisis or difficult situation, try your best to be a blessing.

- If you find yourself in a hospital location, be sure that you share the Gospel with those you come in contact with.

- Don't let the devil defeat you or allow you to charge God foolishly. God's way is perfect, and He makes no mistakes.

- Love your family; never leave their presence without saying, "I love you."

- Love and pray for one another every day. Prayer is a wonderful treasure.

• • •

Today is the tomorrow we hoped for yesterday. Don't waste it!

Moreover it is required in stewards, that a man be found faithful.

—I Corinthians 4:2

CHAPTER TWENTY

Longevity in the Ministry

A HIGHLIGHT OF OUR SUMMER EVENTS is, of course, July 4th. This is always a fun day with our family as we picnic and enjoy the firework displays around the valley. How blessed we are to live in a country where we have freedom. Although we enjoy freedom, we must remember that men gave their lives, the ultimate sacrifice, so that you and I can enjoy freedom today. As Christians, we must remember that the sacrifice of God's Son was given so that we might have eternal life and know beyond a shadow of a doubt that we can go to heaven by accepting Jesus Christ as our personal Savior. This is not a religion but rather the Bible truth with which each of us must come face to face. Religion can never take you to heaven. Only by placing your faith and trust in Jesus, God's Son, can you know for sure that heaven will be your eternal home. If you do not know Jesus Christ as your personal Savior, I would ask you to let someone explain to you how you, too, can be sure of heaven.

. . .

Every year that our church celebrates another anniversary, it does not seem possible that my husband and I have been at North Valley Baptist Church for so many years. What young kids we were when my husband was voted in as pastor here. God has blessed, and we are now reaping the benefits and rewards of having stayed at one church for these many years. The road hasn't been easy and only filled with joy and happiness.

On the contrary, there have been many tears, heartaches, disappointments, shocks, setbacks, deaths, and times of desperate need. You might ask what has kept us going when it would have been easy to quit so many times. Although I have been prone to grumble every now and again about the "asphalt jungle," I am very thankful for where God has placed us. I've had to learn to "bloom where I am planted!" I might prefer grass to concrete and cornfields to traffic, but that is not where God has placed us. I shudder to think where thousands of people from the Bay Area would be, had it not been for the North

Valley Baptist Church. The following has been a help to me, and perhaps it can help you as well, with the idea of sticking with it and staying in the ministry.

- God will never lead us where His grace will not sustain us.

- Family has always been first with us. Although the ministry is of utmost importance, I would never want to lose my family for the sake of the ministry.

- People that are hurting often hurt others. I try to remember that when someone lashes out at my husband, that person probably has a greater need himself.

- When we take our eyes off of God and place them on man, we will always be disappointed.

- If I keep my relationship with God where it needs to be, I will never be overly focused on what people say about me.

- God is always good, in the hard times and in the good times.

- Don't spend time talking about your problems.

- Talk less and listen more.

- Negative people will bring a negative spirit. I cannot allow myself to constantly be thinking on the negative.

- Learn to pray and to praise.

How about you? Are you allowing God to use you where you are? In light of the Lord's imminent return, may each one of us keep on keeping on. Streets of gold, gates of pearl, and mansions of rare beauty will keep us blissfully happy for eternity. The greatest thrill will be to behold the face of our dear Savior and our loved ones awaiting us. Join me in blooming where you are planted today.

It's not worth it to step out of the ministry and lay aside the task that God has called each of us to do. Who will never be reached if you quit the ministry today? Who will step out into eternity never having heard the Gospel of Jesus Christ and perish in hell simply because you quit your race too soon? We must press on and strive to the end, looking for that time when the Lord will call us home.

Favour is deceitful, and beauty is vain: but a woman that feareth the LORD, she shall be praised.

—PROVERBS 31:30

CHAPTER TWENTY-ONE

৩

Once Upon a Time

THAT PERFECT DAY, WITH THE PERFECT man—every girl dreams of her wedding day and being a bride! We plan, prepare, and wish we could go on being a bride forever! The hustle and bustle of planning the picturesquely beautiful wedding becomes overwhelming as brides-to-be are frantically planning and preparing for their dream wedding; while dads are asking, "How much is this going to cost me?!?" Young grooms have fear in their eyes as they price housing and consider just how much their new bride is going to need each week for groceries.

I thoroughly enjoyed planning for the weddings in the Trieber household. For each of our girls, choosing the wedding gown of their dreams was absolutely one of my favorite memories. When I saw Tiffany and Tabitha in their wedding dresses, my eyes welled up with tears; and I couldn't help but think back to their first day of school and the cute little dresses we had picked out for kindergarten. Time passes quickly! Now each wedding dress has been professionally packed away somewhere in both of their homes. I also enjoyed the wedding of our son, Tim. Catching a glimpse of him dressed in his white tuxedo just moments prior to his wedding is something I will keep in my mind's eye forever.

However, it doesn't take long after a wedding is over and the gown is packed away for schedules to become busy, the house to get messy, children to come along, and problems to enter into our lives. Maybe it's time for each of us to go back to the attic, or wherever that wedding dress is stored, and remember some of those promises we made, but perhaps have slowly forgotten in our busyness as wives and mothers.

• • •

The Gown of Commitment

Be committed to being your husband's helper. God gave Eve to Adam to be suitable for him; to complete him, to be his companion, sweetheart, and friend; and to bring him joy and delight.

The Gown of Patience

This is a creation of tribulations, trials and testings. It is the pain that teaches us peace, the trials that teach us tenderness, and the pressures that teach us to have patience.

The Gown of Kindness

Ephesians 4:32 says, "Be ye kind one to another." This gown is soft in texture and is woven together with the threads of gentleness, thoughtfulness, consideration and politeness. The gown of kindness comes in all sizes and features almost unnoticeable details which add character and beauty.

The Gown of Joy

This gown is comfortable and leaves a happy touch whenever it is worn. It is a mood setter. It brings friendly laughter and conversation and leaves out criticisms and harsh words.

The Gown of Trust

This gown is to be worn in place of worry and anxiety. It has a relaxing and calming effect. It is decorated with appliqués of peace, respect, and acceptance. It is good to wear when you are not sure where the money is going to come from or when things are not going so well between you and that teenager you love so much.

The Gown of Endurance

This gown is designed for rugged wear. It will take us through the toughest circumstances. It has features such as faithfulness, tolerance, helpfulness, and steadfastness. I Corinthians 15:58 says, "Therefore, my beloved brethren, be ye stedfast, unmoveable, always abounding in the work of the Lord, forasmuch as ye know that your labour is not in vain in the Lord."

The Gown of Hope

One must never forget to wear the gown of hope. Some of you sweet ladies are clinging to it pretty heavily right now. Hope is manufactured by optimism. It can turn dark, rainy days into sunny ones; and, when worn on days of despair and defeat, you will find that it brings you encouragement.

The Gown of Love

Last, but not least, is the gown of love—and this gown is to be worn all the time. This gown will never fail to heal a wounded marriage or to soothe an aching heart. This gown will never fail to repair the lines of communication and remedy a critical spirit. This gown will bring hope to the hopeless and life to those who are outside of Christ.

So, go ahead . . . take another look at your wedding gown and remember the valuable promises you made "once upon a time!"

He healeth the broken in heart, and bindeth up their wounds.

—PSALM 147:3

CHAPTER TWENTY-TWO

∽

Mending a Broken Heart

DURING 2010, MANY THINGS HAPPENED in my life that were both exciting and wonderful, while others were heart-wrenching and devastating. It is easy to praise God when things go smoothly; but when heartaches and disappointments come, that can be a different story. If you've had one of those "less fortunate" experiences in your life, you know what it's like to have well-meaning people try to cheer you up and give you plenty of advice and, of course, Scripture. While people mean well (and I have done the same thing), quoting Scripture and telling someone that God has everything under control doesn't always bring immediate comfort.

Now, before you say, "Wow, Mrs. Trieber, how unspiritual of you," let me explain. When people have been saved for years and are truly seeking a close relationship with the Lord, they really don't need someone quoting Romans 8:28 to them. They know it is in the Bible and have probably quoted it many times before. People don't need to hear about your experiences and how bad you have or have had it. I know we would all like to think our situation is a " first," but it just isn't so. We've all read the quote, "When life gives you lemons, make lemonade." There's no need to share clichés with a seasoned Christian going through dark days.

Let me share with you what one friend did for me when I was traveling a tough road. She wrote a personal note in her own handwriting (not a text or an e-mail), and simply said: "I know you have gone through some difficult experiences, and although I can't say anything you don't already know, I wanted to let you know that I am praying for you." That was it – cut and dry! I read the note and thought, "No story to share and no list of Psalms or Scriptures to read? That's unusual!" That simple note from a dear friend many miles away made me realize how I needed to be careful with the advice I give and the comments I offer when others are going through hard times.

February is known as national "Love Your Heart" month. You can easily pick up more than one magazine in your local grocery store or Target that will suggest good things to do for your heart like diet, exercise, and supplements that all promise to be heart healthy. Suffering from a broken heart can hurt so deeply that it actually causes your physical heart to hurt. As important as it is to keep your physical heart healthy, we must take every measure to mend our broken hearts and allow the Lord to restore us again. Let me encourage you with this thought: broken hearts do mend even though, at the time, it doesn't seem they ever will. Do what is necessary to help with your heartache—like reading Scripture, praying, or singing songs and hymns. Then, let God do His perfect work in your life. He knows the storm you are facing or are about to face. He knows exactly where you are. Keep your head high and your eyes lifted toward heaven.

Keep in mind that you are not the first to be acquainted with sorrow, grief and pain; and be very careful what you say to others during their difficult times.

*And I thank Christ Jesus our Lord, who hath
enabled me, for that he counted me faithful,
putting me into the ministry.*

—I TIMOTHY 1:12

CHAPTER TWENTY-THREE

After All These Years

AFTER OVER THREE DECADES OF SERVING our Lord in the same place, I have come to learn some things. No, I am not saying I have arrived or that I have nothing left to learn. But, through the years of our ministry, I have learned many a lesson. I hope they are a blessing and help to you as you serve our Lord.

- No Christian lady ever becomes all that she can be until she has a problem that she can share with God alone.

- Troubles and trials are as necessary to our spiritual welfare, just as rain and sunshine are necessary to life. "Yet man is born unto trouble, as the sparks fly upward" (Job 5:7).

- God's grace can meet every need we have, and His grace is always sufficient for every situation.

- See yourself through the eyes of God.

- Friends can make you or break you. Show me your friends, and I will show you your future.

- This modern world is full of sensual, sloppy-looking junk! Please help us bring some class and dignity back to our churches and homes.

- My life will be an example and a story for someone else to tell to others one day.

- We all have a race to run. Don't quit!

- Guard your spirit—your prevailing attitude.

- Be self-motivated. Don't depend on someone else to motivate you.

- Married children still need you! While you want to be sure not to smother, you can still mother.

- You will go through seasons of life. "To every thing there is a season" (Ecclesiastes 3:1).

- You will suffer from bouts of loneliness.

- God made you an original. Don't try to be someone else. It doesn't work.

- A holy life is the result of the inward Christ.

- Completely surrender your will to the Lord.

- Make a big deal over others' birthdays.

- Keep your husband and children first.

- Take an active part in the education of your children. Don't sigh and complain about activities, homework, and sporting events.

- Devotions are necessary for the Christian family, even if they are not always enjoyed all the time. Find something that works for your family.

- Don't forget what it is like to be a kid.

- Be in style! Modesty is always in, but frumpy is not.

- Make your home a haven.

- Exercise. Watch your weight and diet.

- Life is not a dress rehearsal; this is the show.

Thou therefore endure hardness, as a good soldier of Jesus Christ.

—II Timothy 2:3

∽

CHAPTER TWENTY-FOUR

Get Your Game Face On

WE ARE ALL INVOLVED IN A SPIRITUAL battle with an enemy who will never let up. Even though it is people who do evil things to us, we have to keep in mind that it is our ultimate enemy, the devil, who is behind it. Ephesians 6:12 says, "For we wrestle not . . . against powers, against the rulers of the darkness of this world, against spiritual wickedness in high places." Even when we are being attacked by a person, recognizing our real enemy will be the first step in standing strong against him.

Just as God has a plan for you, so does Satan. Satan's plan is to steal from you and destroy your life. He disguises himself to look non threatening and deceives you into thinking that you are not in any danger. He never takes a day off. He is constantly trying to see his plan for your life fulfilled. That is why you have to "Be sober, be vigilant; because your adversary the devil, as a roaring lion, walketh about, seeking whom he may devour" (I Peter 5:8).

For the most part, we are able to recognize obvious attacks of the enemy. But the more subtle ones, when we are being deceived into accepting something into our lives that will ultimately get us off track or destroy us, are harder to recognize. For example, he will attempt to make you believe you deserve every bad thing that happens to you. But deserving is not the issue with God. We didn't deserve to have Jesus die for us; yet He did. The point is not whether we deserve the things the devil throws our way; the point is that Jesus died so we don't have to experience them. How then can we win this battle that we are in every day with the wicked one called Satan?

Be Optimistic

We all have times when we are in season and others when we are out of season. Not everyone is an optimist by nature. My husband is one of the greatest optimists I have ever met. I, on the other hand, have to work at it. It is easier for me to find the bad and praise it. This tendency is something that I have to work on improving all the time. If this is a weakness for you, it can be turned into strength by the Holy Spirit.

Have a Purpose and Determination

Incorporate these into your life every day. Purpose to learn something new each day. Read and study. Do not be a soap opera queen—that's not real life! Neither are fashion magazines or the most popular movie star. Have a purpose to do something that will help you end each day with a sense of accomplishment. Determined people are not easily discouraged. Daniel purposed in his heart that he would not defile himself with the portion of the king's meat or with the wine which he drank. Because he had purposed to do right when the small temptations came, he was able to maintain his purpose to do right when he was faced with a bigger temptation to do wrong.

Don't Be Afraid of a Challenge

A challenge is something that by its nature serves as a test. Determine to go through the testing and come out on the other side. Difficulty will make you a better, stronger Christian. Challenges help us learn as they motivate us to try harder. Challenge is a great deterrent to depression. Facing a challenge keeps you too busy to sit down and be depressed.

Strive for Excellence in Everything You Do

But, don't be defeated when everything is not perfect. You don't always have to measure up to someone else's standard. Be the best you can be even on days when you don't feel your best.

Have Self-Discipline

Reach your goals with self-discipline so that you can help others reach theirs. God's timing is everything. Don't make God fit into your vision—instead, fit yourself into God's vision. Too many people are having visions and wanting God to get into "their plan." Noah didn't one day decide he was going to build an ark and then, after he was finished, ask God to do something with it that would go down in history. Noah walked with God, and God blessed him.

Remember That the Battle Is Not Yours

The battle belongs to God. II Chronicles 20:15 tells us, "Be not afraid nor dismayed by reason of this great multitude; for the battle is not yours, but God's." God is not asking you to be perfect. He is asking you to allow Him to be perfect in you.

It's time to get our game faces on and battle whatever the devil throws our way through the Lord's power.

Who can find a virtuous woman? for her price is far above rubies.

—Proverbs 31:10

∽

CHAPTER TWENTY-FIVE

My Tribute to Mom

OF ALL RELATIONSHIPS IN LIFE, A MOTHER and daughter relationship is one of life's greatest treasures. Having been reared in the home of a pastor and being from a large family of six brothers and one sister, I look back on never quite enough time with just Mom. She was busy raising eight children and being a pastor's wife. I do not remember my mom having time for herself, and I certainly don't remember my mom "spending time with the girls." Mom was a hard worker and a very dedicated wife and mother.

We lived in the church parsonage, which underwent several re-modeling projects to accommodate our large family, and a new church building was under construction to accommodate our growing congregation. It was during this time that my mom was diagnosed with cancer. These were extremely hard days for our family, and if you've ever heard the word "cancer" as a diagnosis for a loved one, you know exactly what I mean.

Oftentimes, as a teenager, I would sit down and write poems to express some thought or emotion I was feeling. I remember the day as though it were yesterday that my mom asked me to write a poem should the Lord decide to take her to heaven. What a request! Little did I know that in a few short months my mom would pass away and I would find myself writing a poem to be read at her funeral service.

Of all the disappointments and sorrows that life can bring, very little can compare to that of losing your mother. Mom never met the man I was to marry and was neither at my wedding nor at the birth of my children. In fact, my mom was only able to attend the wedding of my brother, DeWayne, and she passed away within hours after my brother, Rich was married. For me personally, losing Mom at a young age caused me to try to be the best mom I could be. I know that if you have lost a mother you can be so consumed with the loss that you actually do not concentrate on being a good mother. The passing of my mother has made me determined to be a great mother and nana while I have the opportunity.

The following is the poem that I wrote for my mom in 1970:

A tribute you've asked me to write,
I can well remember the day,
Told me to write a poem to you
When 'ere God called you away.

We never thought our world would be shaken,
That you from us, so soon would be taken.

We've seen it happen to others and tried to understand
Told them God didn't make mistakes
All things by Him were planned.

Though to us it is still unreal,
We prayed that God your body would heal.
But God in His way had a different plan,
So we'll not question but understand.

The memories you've left are precious
Each and everyone,
The joys, the tears, the sorrows, and the
Many battles won.

A faithful wife you've been to Dad
Down through your walk of life,

Shared the burdens of the Church,
The toils and the strife.

Dad's talked so much of his love for you,
How you've been good and kind,
Devoted and so true.

The backbone of his ministry it's often said you've been,
Counselor, laborer and sometimes slave,
For Dad and work, your life you gave.

We children each will miss you,
For us so much you've done.
The problems that you've helped us solve,
Small or great, not one was shunned.

A Christian mother you have been,
Teaching us right from wrong,
Making sure that we were saved
And our faith in God was strong.

You told us not to be bitter,
That God knows what is best,
Read His word and trust in Him,
Upon His promises rest.

So, as we mourn your passing,
The thought of you going away,
Heaven's become more precious
And we're looking for that day;

When at the trump the dead shall rise
Caught up with Him to be,
We'll all be re-united, each other again to see.
The time is quickly passing for God to call us home;
We'll drop our labors, toils and tears,
Never again to roam.

So as we face tomorrow
And the things that it may bring,
We are more than conquerors
And death where is thy sting?

• • •

As a wife and mom myself, it has been my goal to exemplify these characteristics just like Mom did. I hope they will be a help to you as you strive to be the mom and wife you were meant to be. Here are several lessons I learned from my mom.

- Life doesn't always give you everything you want.
- Mom was a hard worker. She didn't know a lot about leisure time.

- She loved her husband and tried to please him in every way she could.

- She loved her children. Although there were a lot of us, we knew Mom loved each one of us for who we were.

- Mom loved people and tried to give of her time to them.

- Mom loved the Lord. I remember catching her reading her Bible and praying. Not long ago, I inherited my mom's Bible from my brother, DeWayne. It is a blessing to look at the markings in her Bible in her own writing and to caress the pages that she touched.

- Mom knew how to have fun and enjoyed making us laugh both by the things she said and did.

- Mom supported my dad in his desire to have family devotions. As children, we certainly didn't always appreciate them, but my mom encouraged Dad. It was during family devotions, with my mom while my dad was out of town, that I accepted Jesus Christ as my personal Savior.

- Mom had a passion for her family.

She was excited about heaven! Her favorite song was "He the Pearly Gates Will Open." I know that God had something very special for Mom to do for Him in heaven and that He took her a little early in order for her to be able to get it all done.

She was a wonderful lady and I miss her very much! If you have lost a mother prematurely, you are not alone. Remember all the good things that your mom did and taught you, and let her live on through you!

ABOUT THE AUTHOR

Born into a pastor's home in Rockford, Illinois, Cindie (Swanson) Trieber has been involved in the Gospel ministry her entire life. In 1972, she married Jack Trieber. They moved to California where he took the pastorate at North Valley Baptist Church, in Santa Clara. For more than thirty-five years, Mrs. Trieber has served in almost every capacity imaginable. After serving as the principal of the North Valley Baptist Schools, which she helped found in 1977, Mrs. Trieber later began her journey as a mother. Her children, Tiffany, Timothy, and Tabitha, are all married and serving full-time in the ministry at North Valley. Within the past few years, the Lord has also blessed Mrs. Trieber and her family with seven (soon to be eight) grandchildren.

From years of experience, Mrs. Trieber possesses a wealth of knowledge and wisdom on how to raise a godly family for Christ, how to love and support a husband, and how to keep a happy and healthy home.

Visit North Valley Publications online
nvpublications.org

Other sites of interest
nvbc.org · knvbc.com · gsbc.edu

Kishwakee Baptist
   Pastor Ford

Cindie's   Grand father